NOISY
POEMS

Collected by
Jill Bennett

Illustrated by
Nick Sharratt

OXFORD

UNIVERSITY PRESS

THE CEREMONIAL BAND

(To be said out loud by a chorus and solo voices)

The old King of Dorchester,
He had a little orchestra,
And never did you hear such a
           ceremonial band.
  'Tootle-too,' said the flute,
  'Deed-a-reedle,' said the fiddle,
For the fiddles and the flutes were
           the finest in the land.

The old King of Dorchester,
He had a little orchestra,
And never did you hear such a
           ceremonial band.
  'Pump-a-rum,' said the drum,
  'Tootle-too,' said the flute,
  'Deed-a-reedle,' said the fiddle,
For the fiddles and the flutes were
           the finest in the land.

The old King of Dorchester,
He had a little orchestra,
And never did you hear such a
           ceremonial band.
  'Pickle-pee,' said the fife,
  'Pump-a-rum,' said the drum,
  'Tootle-too,' said the flute,
  'Deed-a-reedle,' said the fiddle,
For the fiddles and the flutes were
           the finest in the land.

The old King of Dorchester,
He had a little orchestra,
And never did you hear such a
           ceremonial band.
  'Zoomba-zoom,' said the bass,
  'Pickle-pee,' said the fife,
  'Pump-a-rum,' said the drum,
  'Tootle-too,' said the flute,
  'Deed-a-reedle,' said the fiddle,
For the fiddles and the flutes were
           the finest in the land.

The old King of Dorchester,
He had a little orchestra,
And never did you hear such a
           ceremonial band.
  'Pah-pa-rah,' said the trumpet,
  'Zoomba-zoom,' said the bass,
  'Pickle-pee,' said the fife,
  'Pump-a-rum,' said the drum,
  'Tootle-too,' said the flute,
  'Deed-a-reedle,' said the fiddle,
For the fiddles and the flutes were
           the finest in the land,
Oh! the fiddles and the flutes were
           the finest in the land!

James Reeves

ON THE NING NANG NONG

On the Ning Nang Nong
Where the Cows go Bong!
And the Monkeys all say Boo!
There's a Nong Nang Ning
Where the trees go Ping!
And the tea pots Jibber Jabber Joo.
On the Nong Ning Nang
All the mice go Clang!
And you just can't catch 'em when
they do!
So it's Ning Nang Nong!
Cows go Bong!
Nong Nang Ning!
Trees go Ping!
Nong Ning Nang!
The mice go Clang!
What a noisy place to belong,
Is the Ning Nang Ning Nang Nong!

Spike Milligan

SONG OF THE TRAIN

Clickety-clack,
Wheels on the track,
This is the way
They begin the attack:
Click-ety-clack,
Click-ety-clack,
Click-ety, *clack-ety,*
Click-ety
Clack.

Clickety-clack,
Over the crack,
Faster and faster
The song of the track:
Clickety-clack,
Clickety-clack,
Clickety, clackety,
Clackety
Clack.

Riding in front,
Riding in back,
Everyone hears
The song of the track:
Clickety-clack
Clickety-clack,
Clickety-*clickety*
Clackety
Clack.

David McCord

SAMPAN

Waves lap lap
Fish fins clap clap
Brown sails flap flap
Chop-sticks tap tap
Up and down the long green river
Ohe Ohe lanterns quiver
Willow branches brush the river
Ohe Ohe lanterns quiver
Waves lap lap
Fish fins clap clap
Brown sails flap flap
Chop-sticks tap tap

Tao Lang Pee

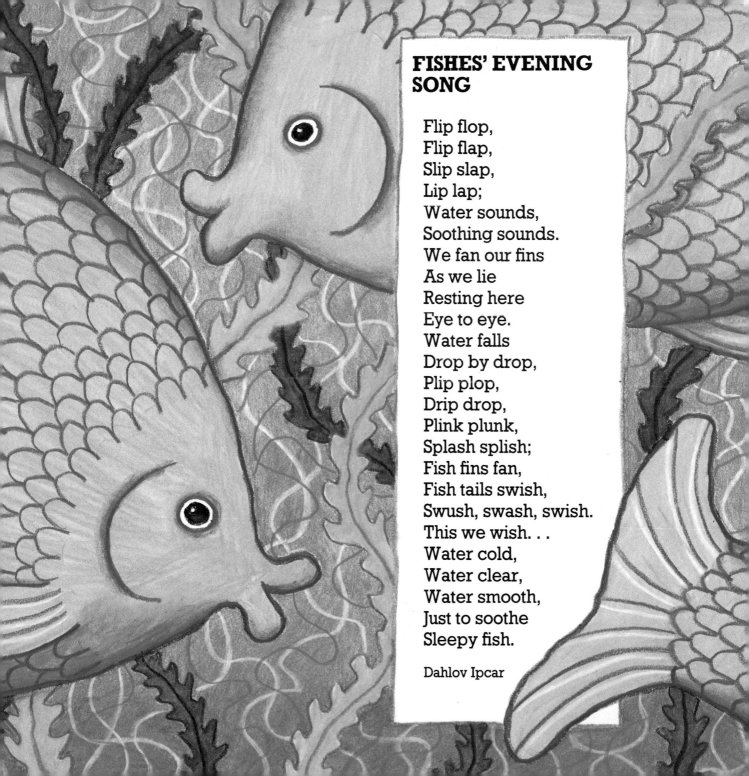

FISHES' EVENING SONG

Flip flop,
Flip flap,
Slip slap,
Lip lap;
Water sounds,
Soothing sounds.
We fan our fins
As we lie
Resting here
Eye to eye.
Water falls
Drop by drop,
Plip plop,
Drip drop,
Plink plunk,
Splash splish;
Fish fins fan,
Fish tails swish,
Swush, swash, swish.
This we wish. . .
Water cold,
Water clear,
Water smooth,
Just to soothe
Sleepy fish.

Dahlov Ipcar

SPAGHETTI! SPAGHETTI!

Spaghetti! spaghetti!
you're wonderful stuff,
I love you, spaghetti,
I can't get enough.
You're covered with sauce
and you're sprinkled with cheese,
spaghetti! spaghetti!
oh, give me some more please.

Spaghetti! spaghetti!
piled high in a mound,
you wiggle, you wriggle,
you squiggle around.
There's slurpy spaghetti
all over my plate,
spaghetti! spaghetti!
I think you are great.

Spaghetti! spaghetti!
I love you a lot,
you're slishy, you're sloshy,
delicious and hot.
I gobble you down
oh, I can't get enough,
spaghetti! spaghetti!
you're wonderful stuff.

Jack Prelutsky

RHYME

I like to see a thunder storm,
   A dunder storm,
    A blunder storm,
I like to see it, black and slow
Come stumbling down the hills.

I like to hear a thunder storm,
A plunder storm,
A wonder storm,
Roar loudly at our little house
And shake the window sills!

Elizabeth Coatsworth

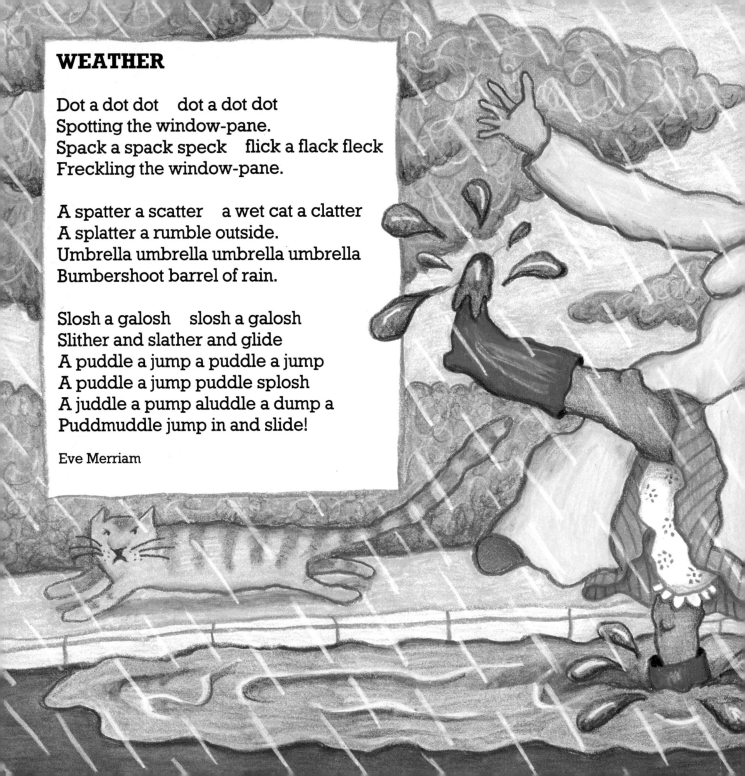

WEATHER

Dot a dot dot   dot a dot dot
Spotting the window-pane.
Spack a spack speck   flick a flack fleck
Freckling the window-pane.

A spatter a scatter   a wet cat a clatter
A splatter a rumble outside.
Umbrella umbrella umbrella umbrella
Bumbershoot barrel of rain.

Slosh a galosh   slosh a galosh
Slither and slather and glide
A puddle a jump a puddle a jump
A puddle a jump puddle splosh
A juddle a pump aluddle a dump a
Puddmuddle jump in and slide!

Eve Merriam

JAZZ-MAN

Crash and
                    CLANG!
Bash and
                    BANG!

And up in the road the Jazz-Man sprang!
The One-Man-Jazz-Band playing in the street,
Drums with his Elbows, Cymbals with his Feet,
Pipes with his Mouth, Accordion with his Hand,
Playing all his Instruments to Beat the Band!

TOOT and
                    Tingle!
HOOT and
                    Jingle!

Oh, what a Clatter! How the tunes all mingle!
Twenty Children couldn't make as much Noise *as*
The Howling Pandemonium of the One-Man-Jazz!

Eleanor Farjeon

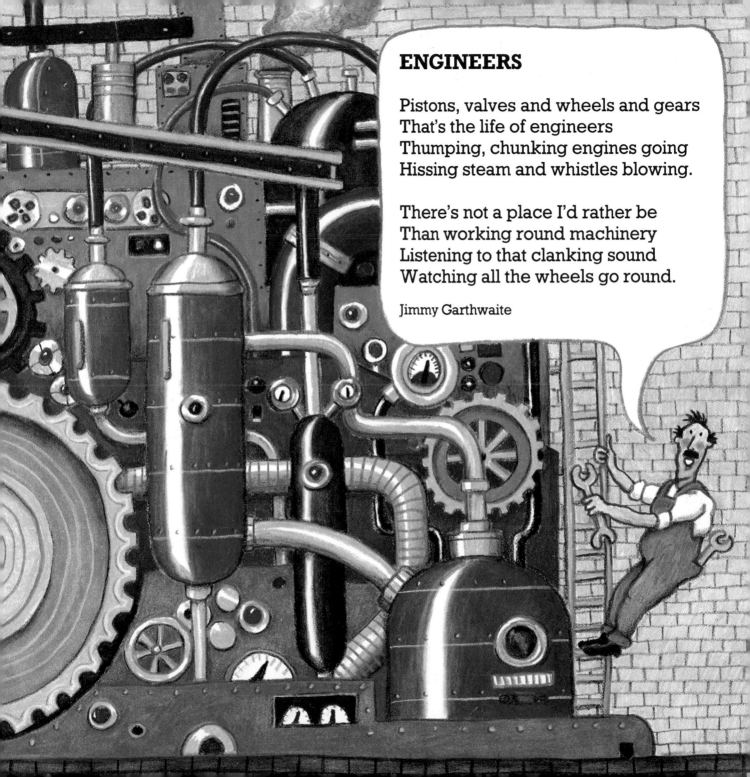

ENGINEERS

Pistons, valves and wheels and gears
That's the life of engineers
Thumping, chunking engines going
Hissing steam and whistles blowing.

There's not a place I'd rather be
Than working round machinery
Listening to that clanking sound
Watching all the wheels go round.

Jimmy Garthwaite

THE YAK

Yickity-yackity, yickity-yak,
the yak has a scriffily, scraffily back;
some yaks are brown yaks and some yaks are black,
yickity-yackity, yickity-yak.

Sniggildy-snaggildy, sniggildy-snag,
the yak is all covered with shiggildy-shag;
he walks with a ziggildy-zaggildy-zag,
sniggildy-snaggildy, sniggildy-snag.

Yickity-yackity, yickity-yak,
the yak has a scriffily, scraffily back;
some yaks are brown yaks and some yaks are black,
yickity-yackity, yickity-yak.

Jack Prelutsky

THE SMALL GHOSTIE

When it's late and it's dark
And everyone sleeps. . . shhh shhh shhh,
Into our kitchen
A small ghostie creeps. . . shhh shhh shhh.

We hear knocking and raps
And then rattles and taps,

Then he clatters and clangs
And he batters and bangs,

And he whistles and yowls
And he screeches and howls. . .

So we pull up our covers over our heads
And we block up our ears and WE STAY IN OUR BEDS

Barbara Ireson

ickety HISS RIGGLE toot TAP HOO plip P EED-

plop rap SPLASH jingle HOOT plip slish slos

ping slosh click knock BANG sniggildy PLINK PLUNK

AR TOOTLE-TOO clap BATTER plop clunk clack toot clap

ping Boo Yickity-yak plip SLIP SLAP rap BOO plop

urp flip BONG toot RATTLE slap

oomba-zoom SLITHER-yak Boo thump slap BONG slosh a galosh

clap shake JIBBER THUNDER clang chop dur

knock GOBBLE clang JABBER plop SLURP BO

flap BANG SCREECH BONG pump-a-rum plip plop ping shigg

TOOT BASH ping JINGLE thump CLANK BONG rap TAP crac

ingle FLICK spatter plop CLANK pickle-pee CLANG

ash HISS clunk A FLACK slosh toot sniggildy-snag BONG SQUI

splish splash BANG HOOT slish CRASH BONG SQUI

SQUIGGLE SWASH thunder HOOT FLIP FLOP clap tootle-too hiss

SNIGGILDY slurp CLICKETY-CLACK YAK slop tap clunk BON

wl slosh ICKITY YAK FLIP plip plop SCREE howl zo

TAP scatter ba ATHER

EDLE toot stumble ZOOMB TAP YO SCU Jibber Ji
atter HOWL tap Flap FLAP rattle slurp Jibber Ju HOWL.
SWISH BOO Flap drip deed-a-ree BOO SLAP
LOW PING splatter TUMBLE TAP SLOSH BONG deed-a-ree BOO swish ziggildy click
wiggle tingle SLOSH BOO dunder dri
SH WHISTLE ROAR click clickety-clack SPLASH SPLISH TAP TA
plop tap ping SLISH bong TAP TAP squiggle clap CLAN
RUMBLE clang drop BANG BASH clap cla
shag ping PUMP-A-RUM SLOSH A GALOSH BONG Flop
H-PA-RAH flip flop slurp SLITHER THUNDER PING bang BOO tingle
slip slap clang WIGGLE plip stumble clatter rat
vl blunder HOOT tootle-too slurp flap TOOT clap PICKLE-PE
LE clunk QUIVER tap tap CRASH HOOT clunk
YOWL rap CLANG SWASH slip slap plip
ckety-clack SCATTER slosh slosh rattle batter TH
ONG clang clap drip drop SWISH Whis
osh YOWL THUMP bber TOO TAP whistle TOOT IGGLE BASH BONG
swish Boo R HOOT SLU pump-a Q